the hygge book

Living a Happy Life the Danish way

Linda Davidsson

Copyright © 2022 by Linda Davidsson

All rights reserved.

No part of this book may be reproduced in any form or by any electronic or mechanical means, including information storage and retrieval systems, without written permission from the author, except for the use of brief quotations in a book review.

contents

Introduction	v
1. HYGGE, WHAT IS IT?	1
2. BRINGING HYGGE INTO THE HOUSE	5
Hygge and Self-Care	11
Hygge and Your Pets	13
3. HYGGE AND YOUR RELATIONSHIP	15
Hygge Date Ideas	18
Indoor Hygge Date Ideas	21
4. USING HYGGE AT WORK	24
Office Space and Desk	27
Alternate Office Space	28
Make Chats Normal	29
Find the Sun	30
5. PARENTING WITH HYGGE	31
Getting Started	32
Danish Parenting	36
What's Not Hygge Parenting?	38
The Benefits	40
6. HYGGE THROUGHOUT THE YEAR	42
Hygge Birthdays	42
Hygge and the Holidays	46
Christmas	49
7. CLOTHING	55
Picking the Best Clothes for a Hygge Winter	58
How to Dress Like a Dane	60
Afterword	65

introduction

Congratulations on purchasing *The Hygge Book,* and thank you for doing so.

The following chapters will discuss the idea of hygge and how you can start implementing this practice into your life.

Hygge may seem like a phase to those who live in countries other than where it originated, but for the Danish people, it is a way of life. When you learn what it is and how to practice it, it can bring peace and calm into your life.

We'll start out by going over what hygge is and a quick little history on it. We don't want to waste too much time here because I'm sure you want to learn how to use hygge.

Then will go into bringing hygge into your home. This will include how to use hygge in your décor, your self-care, and pretty much every other aspect of your home life.

After that, we'll look at how hygge can be brought into your relationships. This is probably one of the most amazing and surprising things about hygge is that it can be used to make healthier relationships.

Next, we'll look at bringing hygge into your work. Just like making your home feel cozy, you can bring that coziness into your job as well.

Then we'll look at how to use hygge to help you as a parent.

Hygge can improve your relationship with your children and help with parenting them.

After that, we'll look at bringing hygge into your life all year long through holidays and other special treatments.

Lastly, we'll look at how to bring hygge into your clothing. We all love to have comfy clothes to relax in, and hygge clothing can help you do just that.

There are plenty of books on this subject on the market; thanks again for choosing this one! Every effort was made to ensure it was full of as much useful information as possible. Please enjoy!

one
hygge, what is it?

HYGGE IS a word that came out of Denmark that is used to acknowledge a moment or feeling. It doesn't even matter if you are with friends or alone, out in public or at home, extraordinary or ordinary as cozy, special, or charming.

Most people pronounce hygge as "hoo-gah," but it is actually pronounced "hue-guh." Hygge or being a "hyggeligt" doesn't mean you have to learn how to do anything. You don't have to change your lifestyle or purchase anything. It isn't a "thing." If anybody tries to tell you something different, they really don't understand this concept. If you were buying things and mentioned what you are doing, they might be trying to get you to buy things that you don't need. You cannot purchase a "hygge room" or "hygge foods."

What does hygge actually mean? Hygge really only takes some slowness, consciousness, and being able to not only be in the present moment but to enjoy and recognize the present. This is why most people explain hygge as being a feeling. If you can't "feel" hygge, you aren't doing it right.

Another way to describe hygge is creating intimacy. This can either be with your home, family, friends, or by yourself. Even though there isn't a simple definition or an English word that can describe hygge, there are many that can be used to describe hygge's idea like simpleness, kinship, reassurance, comfort, familiarity, security, contentedness, happiness, charm, and coziness.

The Danes created this concept since they have had to survive being bored during the cold, dark, long winter months. Even though hygge is a way for them to celebrate every moment, acknowledge, and then be able to break up the harsh and mundane. Since they have so many dark and cold days, just lighting a candle and pouring themselves a cup of hot chocolate makes a huge difference in their spirit.

Through the act of doing simple things, like brewing a cup of tea and pouring it into your favorite teacup, or buying yourself a bouquet of flowers to brighten your home, you can bring hygge into your home. Danish people can see the personal and domestic areas of their life as being an art form, and they don't think that every tiny detail has to be done. They don't try to escape their lives. They embrace every single aspect of life to the fullest. They put hygge into each day, so it is just another extension instead of being a stressed or forced event.

They can turn the word coffee into a verb by making a ritual of brewing it each morning. Having a cozy evening at home with friends and just enjoying one another's company or lighting a candle for every meal, hygge is more about being aware of every moment and making it great. Hygge is simplicity. Outsiders have a hard time understanding this simplicity.

Hygge is more about getting away from the daily grind to be with the people you love or just by yourself while relaxing and enjoying all of life's pleasures.

Hygge, the word, can be dated back to about 1800, well, for the meaning as we know it now. Different definitions of hygge date back all the way to the Middle Ages. There was an Old Norse word that meant "protected from the outside world."

Hygge can be about time together that is informally shared with close friends and family. Normally, the setting will be in a quiet location, whether it is in your home or a picnic in the park on a warm summer day. It normally involves sharing a bowl of candy, a cup of hot chocolate, a beer, a glass of wine, or a meal. There won't be any agenda because you are just celebrating the joys of life, or you might decide to discuss deep topics. It is a chance to take things slow and unwind.

- Pop Culture and Products

Merchandisers and designers have moved fast to cash in on this new hygge concept. You can find books about hygge, so-called hygge housewares like candles and fluffy blankets. You can also find hygge clothes like a soft, warm sweater. The softness and warmth of a sweater can put you in a wonderful, calming mood.

- Hygge and Tourism

Anyone who visits Denmark seems to always ask for a "taste of hygge." Even though hygge is hard to reach if you aren't surrounded by familiar things and friends, having a hearty dinner in a restaurant located inside an old building with candles glowing is a great way to begin. Strolling through the Tivoli Gardens amusement park located in Copenhagen on a warm, sunny day or walking with a friend on the beach of Jutland can create hygge.

Hygge is thought of as everyone being equal, even if there is an imbalance of power.

- Why Danes Love Hygge

The wet, dark, and cold climate during the long winter months have encouraged Danes to spend more time indoors together. Winter is the best time to experience hygge.

There are other factors that come into play, too. Hygge is a reflection of the Danish society's values of equality and making sure everyone is doing well. They always try to make sure that everyone is treated well and arguments normally don't happen during moments of hygge because nobody wants to waste the positive energy.

Even though hygge could be extremely rejuvenating and enjoyable, it is also an exercise that could leave people who are just visiting Denmark for the first time standing on the outside looking in. Hygge helps people to enclose, cluster, and shelter. It might be hard for outsiders to have access to any occasion where hygge just happens.

two
bringing hygge into the house

IN THE SCANDINAVIAN way of life that is hygge, it is meant to help bring calm and warmth into your life. It is a celebration of happiness and health, and you can bring it into your home in many different ways. Décor is one of them. You can easily bring hygge into your home by:

- Enjoying a book
- Appreciating your surroundings
- Taking up a new hobby
- Reuse and recycle
- Barbeque outside
- Stay in bed for an extra hour
- Be present and thankful
- Enjoying the simple pleasures
- Surrounding yourself with family and friends

Let's take a look at some ways that you can decorate your home to embody hygge. With hygge, you want to create a safe space for you and your family to live in. When decorating, you want to keep things as simple as possible to immerse yourself into this cozy and carefree life.

A hygge home is an environment that speaks to the soul and brings warmth to the lives of all who enter your front door. We all know those people who work hard to keep their homes styled with the latest trends, but those come and go. Instead, try decorating your home the hygge way. This will make your home cozy, and cozy is something that lasts forever.

- Pick neutral color schemes

When it comes to picking out a color scheme for your home décor, you don't want it to become too overwhelming. The things that you add to your home should add to a feeling of peace and harmony. By sticking to a neutral palette, you can help create a relaxing space. Creams, browns, light grays, and pastel colors help to create a comfortable area.

- Create a comfortable space

Making your home feel cozy is one of the most important parts of hygge décor. A great way to bring comfortableness into your home is by using fluffy pillows and soft blankets. Getting to snuggle on the couch with pillows and blankets gives you a great place to unwind after a long day. Something that would be fun if you have the space is to create a cozy nook on a love seat or a window bench. These are great places for your relaxation with some hot cocoa and a good book for a little quiet time.

- Library and books

There is no need to have a whole room dedicated to books to bring a library into your home. All you need is a small shelf or several bookshelves to create a space to house your favorite books. I believe that you can look at a person's bookshelf and know more about them in a few minutes than after having an hour-long conversation. It doesn't matter what books you bring into your home. Get what you like, whether their cookbooks, memoirs, or novels. Books should be center stage in a hygge home.

You can also create a "Free Library" in front of your home. This is simply a book exchange for the neighborhood. This is a great thing to have for children and adults alike.

- Bring in nature

Whether it's the summer or the winter, you can bring nature inside by using natural elements. Wood is a great material to use in your home that will help to bring nature inside for a happier and cozier feel. Wood décor, floors, and furniture help bring us closer to nature. This is an important aspect of hygge. You can also bring in plants, unfinished wood, and clay pieces.

- Candles

When you think about candles, what is one of the first things that you think of? Maybe you think of romance, or you could see yourself laying in a warm bath, or even a calm night enjoyed in the company of a good book. All of these things encompass the idea of hygge. The soft glow of a candle can't be created by anything else and can easily be used in any area of your home.

- Twinkly lights

Twinkly lights are a great way to bring hygge into your home. They are festive and cheery, and they look amazing anywhere. They can be set up in the living room, bedroom, bathroom, and even on your patio. Much like candles, they provide softer light and add a pleasant atmosphere to your home without becoming overwhelming.

- Natural lighting

Candles and twinkle lights are great soft lighting options for the evening and night hours, but during the day, you should try to bring in some natural light. The natural light will help boost your vitamin D, which will improve your mood. If you don't have a lot of windows in your home, you can hang a mirror on the wall opposite of window to bring in more light and make your space feel bigger.

- Make a fire

Getting to huddle up next to a fire, whether inside or outside, is a big part of Danish culture. Fires create a place to gather with your family and friends and be thankful. While not everybody can have a fireplace, for those who do, use it to bring more hygge into your life. Even an outdoor fire pit is a great thing to have.

- Add texture

When it comes to cozy décor, the texture might not be the first thing you think of. However, bringing texture into your living space is an amazing way to add interest to what tends to be a more minimalist design. This can be done by incorporating natural, warm materials like wool and wood into your home. To add a pop of color to your home, you can use a variety of different flowers.

- Add nostalgia

Hygge is all about feelings of happiness, and what better way than adding décor that evokes feelings of nostalgia. These could be photos of your loved ones, a blanket that reminds you of somebody or your childhood, or even a certain scent that reminds you of your favorite time of year.

- Create a spa bathroom

Instead of your bathroom being a place that you take a quick shower in each morning, make it a relaxing point in your home. You want your bathroom to be a place where you can rejuvenate and rest. To make a bathroom that is peaceful and pleasant, ensure that you have plenty of storage space to avoid a bunch of clutter. You can even add some fluffy robes and candles to give a serene, laidback environment.

- A welcome mat

What is more inviting than a welcome mat at your front door. You may have a crazy, hectic day, but when you get to come home, and you have the right welcome mat, it will let you know that you are back at your hygge haven. The welcome mat can be changed throughout the year to match the seasons to give your home the right look.

- Hygge art

Getting things for you home that an artist has poured their heart into is very much hygge approved. Whether this is through woodwork, weavings, handmade quilts, pottery, sculpture, prints, or paintings, each one of them adds more warmth to your home. Finding time-worn vintage paintings is a great aesthetic to add to your home if you are into weathered items.

- Baskets

Having baskets in your home not only helps bring natural elements inside, but they are functional as well. You can store items in baskets, and they look great.

- Rugs

A great element to add a feeling of coziness to your home is a rug. They help by adding a pop of color to your home, as well as bringing in a warm texture. Rugs are a great way to define a space in your home. Adding a plush rug to an otherwise dead space is great to liven it up. For those with tiled or wood flooring, a rug can act as a sound absorber.

So, how can you know what elements you should add to your home? Whether you like industrial, bohemian, Scandinavian, coastal, Shabby Chic, French Country, rustic, traditional, country, minimalist, modern, cottage, English cottage, or modern farmhouse décor styles, you can add in cozy elements to all. Here's a little exercise to get your mind in the right space for picking out your hygge décor.

Picture yourself in your home. There is snow falling outside your window, and you are fixing stew on the stove. There is the smell of baking bread in the air. Your table is set with some candles because your friends are coming over to have dinner. As you look around your home, there is a feeling of warmth because you know that you have created your home with love. This is a hygge home.

Now, take a moment to write down everything that you imagined your home looked like in that mental picture. What types of things did you feel when you pictured your home? That is what your vision of a hygge home should be. Now it is your turn to bring that idea of a perfect hygge home to life.

Keep in mind that hygge isn't just about trying to get your home decorated to perfection. Instead, it's all about finding things that mean something to you, remind you of special moments, inspire you, and give you a space that you can share with people you love. A hygge home doesn't need to be a perfect home. It's a cozy and happy home.

Hygge and Self-Care

Hygge can be brought into your life through self-care practices as well. It's all about making yourself feel good, so let's look at some self-care practices that can bring more hygge into your life.

- Warm lemon water

Warm drinks on a cool day are great. Warm lemon water has a bunch of health benefits, especially when you make a point of drinking a glass each morning. It can help promote skin health and boost your immune system. By adding this simple and effective drink into your life is an easy way to care for your body.

- Slippers

What is cozier than slipping your tired feet into a fluffy pair of slippers at the end of the day. You can also place a basket of slippers by the door in various sizes for your guests. This allows them to take off the, possibly dirty, outside shoes and cover their feet if they aren't comfortable going barefoot in your home. It also keeps your feet warm during the cooler part of the year, which is always nice.

- Bath time

Instead of taking a shower every day, make a point of taking a bath at least once a week. Baths are great for your joints and muscles. Plus, getting to soak your whole body in water also helps with hydration. Add in some soothing music and essential oils to create an extra cozy touch.

- Essential oils

There are numerous benefits that essential oils have. From energy support and stress relief to improving sleep and reducing inflammation, there are a number of benefits of adding essential oils into your routine. You can even diffuse essential oil blends to bring more of the season into your home.

- Make your own food

You never know what has been added to take-out food, so taking the time to make your own food is a great way to bring hygge into your life. Schedule yourself some time to make your own meals with ingredients that you know. Soups are a great soothing meal.

Hygge and Your Pets

Who has more of a hygge life than pets that get to sleep in fluffy beds all day long and don't have anything to worry about except when their human is going to feed them? Hygge can be much more than just creating a warm, nice atmosphere in your home. It's all about enjoying the good moments in your life with your family, friends, and even your pets.

Whether you have a cat, dog, or any other pet, enjoy life with them. Whether that means you play with your cat as you make some coffee or petting your dog as you relax on the couch. Your pets can bring so much calmness into your life if you let them.

To help you bring your pets into your hygge lifestyle, here are some simple steps:

1. When you have some free time, turn off your electronics or remove them from the room.
2. Light some candles and get your room as dimly lit as possible.
3. Make some tea or hot chocolate or your other favorite warm beverage, and invite your cat or dog to come over and cuddle with you.

4. By petting your pet, you can lower your blood pressure.
5. Feel your pet's heartbeat and use this sound to clear your mind.
6. Cover both of you with a warm blanket and drift off.

The possibilities are endless when it comes to bringing your pets into your life of hygge.

three
hygge and your relationship

HYGGE CAN BE a part of every aspect of your life, from trying to have balance daily, having easy moments with family and friends, treating yourself to your favorite food, and taking the time to enjoy all the simple things.

Here are a few ways you can bring hygge to your relationship and home.

- Get Rid of Clutter

Yes, the homes in Denmark are well-lit and cozy, but there is a reason why they are very sparse. Danish people will tell you that clutter can cause more clutter, and this can lead to arguments over who will clean up the clutter. If you want to find peace in your home, you have to keep the clutter out of your home.

- Make a Playlist

The Danish people will always have the best music playing. They never wait for a BBQ or dinner party to bring out the music. They just play music all the time. They always know just how to create the perfect mood.

- Sacred Dinners

Danish people have always been focused on family meals. They think that dinner is a sacred time. It is the main reason that many offices end their workday by four or five so that they can get home to eat dinner with the family.

Making a special place for the family so they can enjoy their dinner where there aren't any distractions or screens is just as important as making the family content. Hygge experts are extremely strict about always having candles lit on the dinner table, and nobody will have their phone at the table.

- Mix the New and Old

Young people as well and the older people in Denmark are extremely superstitious. Shop owners believe that the objects they sell have souls, and they can have large impacts on the way you feel in your home and the way a couple will relate to each other.

They will encourage you to bring together the old and new. Find some new things that you truly like and add them to the things that have meaning from your past. The main goal here is to combine them in your new home to create a blending of your shared present and your pasts.

- Lots and Lots of Pillows

On a trip to Denmark, we decided to do a little shopping to bring some true Denmark hygge into our new home. We found a cute wooden birdcage that held toilet paper, a garlic press that was more elegant than everything I owned, and a set of pillows that the owner of the shop said would make our living room feel and look amazing and trust me, they did.

In every shop, you will find pillows. Pillows that were sewn by hand with intricate Scandinavian designs on them, pillows made out of Tibetan yak's wool, and pillows created out of upcycled rags and denim. We even saw a pillow adorned with a horse who was wearing a dress. It is amazing how pillows can change a living space. They might just be small things, but sometimes it is the smaller things in life that make the biggest difference.

- Don't Purchase A Lot of Stuff

You don't have to go on a shopping spree to try and fill up your space with fluffy things. I had a shop worker laugh at me as I tripped over things in her shop while trying to carry an armload of pillows plus a blanket that I planned on using to hide a wine stain on my sofa.

After she helped me through the shop, she asked if I was buying gifts for family and friends and I said: "I was buying hygge." She laughed at me again and shook her head. "You can't buy hygge."

She told me that I needed to wait until I found the pieces that talked to me. By doing this, you will appreciate the objects a lot more.

- Remain At Home

Once I moved into my own apartment, I was working countless hours. We live in a society that tells us we need to be in the office all the time in order to make it in this world. There are so many people working who remain "on" when they get home. They sacrifice so much quality time with their significant other.

Since I had moved into my apartment, I have only spent about half my time there. Even if I wasn't traveling for work, I was pathologically and frenetically busy. It was not healthy for me or my relationship to feel as if I was living in a hotel instead of my own place. My significant other and I felt like strangers passing through a shared space.

Hygge experts will tell you that true hygge and true happiness can only be found once you slow down and take the time to be together in your shared space instead of using it as a place to sleep between adventures and meetings.

- Be Happy, Get Cozy

Most people in Denmark stay a lot indoors. This is due to their constantly changing weather. Having a cozy home that is relaxing and personal helps you feel so much better.

Many people might argue that people are trying to make an "invisible" cozy spirit that is supposed to embody hygge in their home since they need a relaxing place. If you are lucky enough to walk into a home and it immediately feels cozy, you have truly entered a hygge home. You will feel wonderful happy energy that will brighten your day. If you feel happy when you get home from work, it will rub off on your significant other.

Hygge Date Ideas

Hygge means many different things to the Danish people. If you ask several people what hygge means to them, you are going to get a different answer from everyone. One person might tell you that hygge is cooking with family. Another will tell you that it is candles burning on the dinner table. Others might say it is enjoying that first cup of coffee sitting by the fireplace.

In its essence, hygge basically embodies anything that brings happiness, contentment, coziness, and warmth into your home. Hygge mainly involves having a good time with the people you love along with some good conversations and great food.

The emphasis needs to be on making an atmosphere that makes you slow down, enjoy every moment, and relax. Everybody can use a bit of hygge, especially people who want to wind down and enjoy a cozy night with your love. Hygge could have a huge impact on your relationship.

- Hygge's Historical Context

Hygge was derived from the Norwegian word "hugga," which basically means "to console" or "to comfort." A literal translation in English would basically mean "a hug."

Most countries in Scandinavia will have their own unique concept about what hygge is. In Sweden, it is called "lagom," which means "adequate" or "just enough." In Norway, it is called koselig.

(Check out my book called *The Lagom Book* for a more in-depth look of this fascinating subject).

Denmark has winters that are bone-chilling. The sun will literally disappear for days on end. In ancient times, during the long winter months, Danish people would rely on activities in their homes to keep them entertained, comfortable, and warm. This is how hygge became an integral part of their culture.

- Popularity of Hygge

Denmark is considered the happiest country in the world. Every Nordic nation is ranked high on the "Human Development Index," and this is why their way of life has made other people so curious about them. Hygge plays a big role in this.

Just think about this, all the Nordic countries will have horrendous winters, and their weather is known to change at a moment's notice. During the long winter months, the sun won't come out for days, and then they have the phenomenon of the midnight sun during the summer when some towns will have sunlight constantly for days.

Just think about how hard it would be to go to sleep with sunlight blaring into your bedroom windows. Because of all these unique weather conditions, Nordic people are at a higher risk of developing SAD or seasonal affective disorder.

But the Nordic people have taken their weather conditions in their stride and built a wonderful quality of life for themselves; this includes paid maternity leave for both parents, social security, a well-planned infrastructure, and a wonderful healthcare system.

For the Danes and all the other Nordic people, hygge is just a natural part of their lives; it is something that they try to keep throughout their entire lives.

- How Hygge Can Improve Your Relationships

In this changing world, our emotions are extremely complex. We can be easily offended, get angry, and most people value our social media likes and comment more than life itself. Don't misunderstand me; technology has brought the world to our fingertips, but it has caused too many distractions, and this makes us less self-aware.

All of these things have changed our relationships. We get upset over the smallest of problems, we don't have a lot of meaning to our relationships, and we break up a lot. Our lives are just too busy to find pleasure in all the little things, such as having a great conversation without picking up your phone once or families talking around the dinner table.

Hygge can be a type of self-care and gives you lessons about how to be mindful. It could help you create deeper bonds with your family or partner. It can teach you to love yourself and appreciate your life by being present in every moment.

- Hygge Isn't New

Many people know about hygge and have experienced some content and warm moments at some time in your life. Here are some instances of cozy moments that you might be familiar with:

1. Enjoying a nice dinner with your family by the fireplace
2. Walking through crunchy leaves
3. Dancing in the rain
4. Cloud watching
5. Curling your toes in the warm sand at the beach

6. Reading a book while snuggled under your favorite blanket
7. Sipping a cup of hot chocolate
8. Enjoying your favorite movie while cuddling up with your significant other

This list could go on, but I think you know where I'm coming from. But you might be thinking... "I do this every Saturday or Sunday, so why is this hygge so special?" The biggest difference is intention. The Danish people look forward to creating an environment that is harmonious, full of coziness and warmth, without any distractions.

Now, think back to some of the moments I mentioned above; how many times were you truly present in those moments without thinking or being stressed about many other things?

Indoor Hygge Date Ideas

- Making Some Ambience

Hygge will never be complicated. All you need is simplicity, company, and comfort. Some hygge date ideas might be wonderful for you and your significant other, and it just might improve many aspects of your relationship, such as teamwork and communication. Below you will find some indoor dates that you can try.

The hygge concept is mainly centered around winter, and most of the ideas you will find in this section might be perfect for a cold winter's night. You could try these in any season; you just might need to adjust some things but never change any of the basic concepts about simplicity, company, and comfort.

- Use Soft Light to Light Up A Cozy Nook

You can easily make a cozy corner where you can curl up with your significant other in the middle of piles of fuzzy blankets and soft pillows. Because lighting is very important when creating a hygge atmosphere, use some soothing "fairy lights" that won't be too harsh on your eyes, and that can help make the atmosphere more romantic.

Put on something that is extremely comfortable, even if it is your favorite pair of ratty sweats that you swear you are going to get rid of, but you haven't yet. Before you say no, your significant other won't be judging you because they will be in their comfy old sweats, too. You can pair these with chunky sweaters and some thick socks if you want to.

- Watch Classic Noir

If you can find some Nordic Noir on Netflix, you are all set. Nordic Noir is legendary. I am not exaggerating either. They are that great, and you will soon be addicted. Watching a great thriller while cuddled under a cozy blanket wrapped in your lover's arms is the best place to be. If you are wondering where to begin, check out *Equinox, The Killing, Young Wallander,* and *The Bridge.*

- Read A Book

You will get brownie points if you can find some Nordic literature. This genre of books is very vast, and most people don't even know that it exists. From mythology to thrillers to contemporary literature, you will be amazed at all the things you can learn about this culture. If you and your significant other love to read, you will enjoy adding to your knowledge about the Nordic heritage. Here are my recommendations:

1. *The Girl With The Dragon Tattoo*
2. *The Poetic Edda: Stories of the Norse God and Heroes*
3. *A Man Called Ove*

- Talk By Candlelight

Candles can always add another dimension to any date night. It makes things more romantic, too. If at all possible, try to light as many as you can. Try to go for the more natural unscented one, so the smells don't get too much. You could use some hygge lamps.

Now, grab a couple mugs of hot cocoa or coffee, turn your phone off or put them in another room, and grab your favorite blanket, wrap yourself up in the blanket and get ready for a great conversation.

- Using Plants To Brighten Your Space

You can create a wonderful atmosphere inside your house by getting some indoor plants like succulents. Philodendron and Monstera are very low maintenance. Just be careful if you have pets, as philodendron is highly toxic. In fact, if you have pets do some research to find plants that are pet friendly. I have a cat who will chew on anything that is green. Plants have the ability to soothe your mind while brightening up your space.

Other than plants, you can use wildflowers, sheer curtains, and vibrant pieces of art which can create a happy environment for your home.

There are good reasons why the Nordic nations are at the top of the list of the happiest countries in the whole world. It is because they always make happiness a priority by only focusing on the simple things in their lives. If you want to make your relationship stronger, take some of the above ideas and focus on having a cozy night with your significant other.

four
using hygge at work

WHEN THE WEEKEND comes to an end, it can cause you to start feeling sad because you know the next day you're going to have to go to work. However, with the knowledge of hygge and a positive mindset, you can make Mondays not so bad. It is fairly easy to create a feeling of security, wellbeing, and comfort when you are at home. However, the workplace is often the area that could use hygge the most. Heading into a nine-hour shift feeling drowsy and without any passion isn't going to make for a great day.

The good news is that you can easily bring hygge into your workspace. Please keep in mind, some of these things may need to be approved by your boss. There is no need to get into trouble for the sake of hygge. However, there should be suggestions that shouldn't need approval.

- Bring your favorite mug

Keeping a warm beverage that you can sip on during the day, even during the summer, can be comforting. Caffeine is also a great way to keep your energy up and help you stay focused. You can even create some camaraderie with your coworkers by having a cup of coffee with them and chatting about something that is non-work-related.

Using your favorite mug is like bringing a little piece home to work with you. It also doesn't hurt getting up to get a refill. This will give your brain a little break from all of your mundane tasks.

- Have a relaxing work playlist

Music can help your mind a lot. Creating a playlist of music that is upbeat but also calming, such as acoustic songs, can help you work through your day. Spotify and iTunes also have hygge playlists that you can choose from. Put on some headphones and zone into your work with the help of some music.

- Have lunch outside and unwind

When you get a lunch break, make a point of actually taking a break. Don't start checking your emails, working on another assignment, or start at your computer as you eat a lackluster sandwich.

If the weather is nice, head outside to get some fresh air. Depending on the location of your work, you could walk to a restaurant to get some lunch or enjoy your packed lunch on a park bench. Whatever you choose to do doesn't matter as long as you go outside and allow yourself to have some time away from work. This could help lift your spirits and get you through that afternoon slump.

- Decorate your workspace

It's helpful to have some personal items. This could be some flowers or pictures of your family. Some string lights draped around your cubicle could be nice. You can also bring in some of your favorite tea that you enjoy during the day as well. As long as you stay within company policy, don't be afraid to move away from what others see as normal.

Instead of viewing this space as a mundane area, you want to make it a comfortable space that will inspire productivity. If your job allows it, you could even bring in an unscented candle. Having a cozy chair and sentimental items can also be helpful.

- Have a potluck

Comfort food is a great source of hygge, and who wouldn't want to get to enjoy some home-cooked meals at work with your coworkers and friends. A big part of Danish culture is having friendly gatherings that involve food. Everybody who wants to can bring in their favorite home-cooked meal, and you can enjoy trying each other's foods together during lunch.

Eating together promotes feelings of hygge and could bring your closer together with your coworkers. Make sure you organize potluck day with everybody so that those who want to participate will know in enough time to bring something in.

- Random acts of kindness

Doing random nice things for your coworkers can bring a feel of hygge to the office. This could be bringing in a box of donuts or complimenting a coworker. This could end up turning their entire day around.

Social support is a great way to deal with stress. Knowing that there are people who care about us can make us happier and more resilient to the stress of life.

- Teamwork

Teamwork is a big part of Danish culture. From a young age, they are taught how to work in groups and seek out or give help when needed. They are encouraged to still feel confident in their abilities despite their need for help.

Maybe you could speak to your supervisor about organizing team-building activities to help you all work better together. You could even have scavenger hunt tournaments to add some fun to the office life.

Alright, with these seven basic tips for adding hygge to your work life, let's break things down a bit further.

Office Space and Desk

There are obvious changes that could be made to an office space to make it cozier, presuming you don't tick off any of your coworkers or break any rules. Try some of these on for size.

1. Place a lamp on your desk with an incandescent bulb to help counteract the fluorescents that are overhead. It will also help counteract the blue light from your computer.
2. Place a cushy jacket or scarf on the back of your chair to help deal with the stiff chairs and cool office temperatures. You could even place the jacket or scarf over your lap to act as a blanket.
3. Wear more comfortable shoes at work. There's a good chance that nobody will really notice if you happen to not be wearing heels or other painful shoes at work.
4. Find some noise that works for you. I mentioned a hygge playlist earlier on, but maybe that's not your cup of tea. You might prefer to listen to some form of white noise. These can be comforting and can also help you focus.
5. Bring plants in. Some succulent plants on your desk are a great way to bring color and nature to your workspace. Plus, succulents are pretty easy to care for.

Alternate Office Space

If you work for a place that is supportive and trusts that you will work even if you aren't at a desk, try out some alternate areas to give yourself a chance.

1. If the place you work is spacious and open-concept, make or find an area that is more intimate. Pull up a comfy chair close to a bookshelf, or see if there is an empty office or room where you could go and work every now and then.
2. Switch up the meeting location. If you don't need a bunch of conference technology, have your team

meet up in a café or a common area. Use a smaller table so that everybody can sit closer together and hear each other better.

Make Chats Normal

Personal connection is an important part of hygge, but it can be something that people aren't comfortable with either. For those who are more introverted, going out of their way to talk to people can be terrifying. However, finding ways to talk and connect with your co-works is important.

1. Schedule a weekly check-in with the coworkers that you are closest to. This will ensure that you stay connected, even when things become hectic. These are the people who you enjoy being around and cheer you on.
2. For coworkers that you would like to know better, invite them for a half-hour one-on-one chat. Maybe you meet up in the break room, over a cup of coffee, or even via Skype. There doesn't need to be any type of agenda, but do think about some things to talk about so that the conversation doesn't lag.
3. Remember the remote coworkers you have. They probably need help maintaining and making connections with their coworkers, so reach out to them.
4. Create a tea station. This is a great way to connect and chat with coworkers when you aren't comfortable with scheduled chat time. You can even get your coworkers involved in setting this up. Grab a clear jar from the dollar store, some tea infusers, mugs, and a French press. This can help you create a hot beverage station, and it will likely come in under

$15. Everybody can pitch in by bringing in their favorite teas or other hot beverages. The key here is to let everybody share, so no names on boxes of tea.
5. Take your coffee or tea break at the same time each day. This will let your coworkers know that is the best time to wander over to you and talk.

Find the Sun

Depending on what time of year it is, you could be commuting home in the dark or in the bright sun. Either way, you can keep yourself from falling into a funk by scheduling time to spend in the daylight.

1. Remember to take your lunch break and head outside. That's the best way to get some sunshine in.
2. Make a few adjustments to your commute to see if you can get some daylight out of the trip. You could always park a little further away from the door so that you get a little sunshine walk in as you head into work.
3. If your job allows it, take a break. Walk outside for five or ten minutes if you can, grab a cup of coffee, or walk around the block.

With these tips in mind, you should be able to bring a bit more hygge into your work life. Maybe, you may find that Mondays aren't so bad.

five
parenting with hygge

THE MOST IMPORTANT part of hygge is spending quality time with those you care about and love. It's that homeyness that you feel when you have that perfect night in. When it comes to how it can affect parenting, it places a lot of importance on bonding with your children in a way that doesn't require an agenda or schedule. You get to enjoy the time that you spend together.

To use hygge in parenting means that you work on creating a comfortable, safe, judgment-free area of togetherness. This can have a huge impact on your children. It gives them the safe space they need to feel as though they can express themselves and strengthen the bond you have with them while also helping them to work through tough emotions, feel secure in themselves, and navigate the changes that occur through childhood.

Besides making sure that you create a safe space for your children, hygge parenting is all about the "we" time. As important as it is to ensure you take time for yourself, it's also important to make sure that you spend time with your children that are free of distractions so that you can focus on them. That's when your relationship with your child will grow.

Getting Started

The first important part of hygge parenting is that your entire lifestyle doesn't have to be changed. Getting into the habit of having those hygge moments is all that you have to do, whether that is once a week, once a day, or even more, as long as you make a point of having those moments with your children. However often you choose to do it, ensure that it is done with intention and that everybody is fully present. Get rid of any distractions and focus on the time that you are spending together.

Start by setting up a cozy atmosphere for these moments you will have with your family. This coziness should be unique to your family. Maybe everybody gets their most comfy pillows and creates a blanket fort to hang out in. If everybody has a bunch of cozy socks, you can each pick out your favorite pair and put them on. Whatever your family finds fun and cozy, that's how you should create your hygge family time. Make sure you get the lighting just right, too. Turn down your lights and maybe light some candles to help up the coziness.

You also need to make it understood that all uncomfortable topics, personal drama, and controversies should be left at the door. This is not the time to hash through those. This is a time to spend with your family and embrace all of the happiness in your life. Even if you're just letting go of those negative things momentarily, it can help you feel grateful for the things you have in life.

- It should be a point, not an accident

It's important to understand that hygge will not come naturally. With everything we have to do in life, and what our kids have to do, homework, housework, and more, hygge can easily find itself on the back burner. That's what you, as the adult, come into play. You have to decide when you want to have a hygge evening, and purposefully get rid of competing interests and distractions. At first, you may have to block out a couple of hours each week. You may already be in the habit of having some hygge time each evening, and if so, then great.

- Make a meeting space comfortable

A big part of hygge is being comfortable. This means that not everybody is going to enjoy sitting down on the hard floor to play a game. Have some blankets, stuffed animals, pillows, and the like to make things more comfortable. If you make the same setup for every hygge moment, your family will start to associate that with your night together. It will go a long way to setting the right tone for the night.

- Lighting

Lighting is a big thing when it comes to talking about hygge. We've already mentioned it several times in this book. Having warm lighting in small areas of your home is preferable to overturning bright fluorescent lights. Candles are one of the best ways to do this. However, if you have small children, you may be concerned about the fire hazard candles present. In that case, you can find inexpensive battery-powered candles. While they may not create the same ambiance as a real candle, it does create a low, safe lighting alternative.

- Get rid of your phone

The phone is one of the biggest sources of distraction. It pulls us into what we think is "urgent," which most of the time it isn't. Then we end up feeling guilty and empty for all of the time that the phone has pulled us away from our family. For the hygge evenings you have planned, you will need to get rid of the computers, phones, and tablets. You can, however, do a movie night because you can still spend time together while cuddled on the couch or floor, enjoying a movie you all love.

- Be present

The main goal of your hygge night should be that you bond with your family. To help maximize the time you spend with them, you need to focus on them. Be completely present. Listen to what they say. Ask them questions, and give them answers if they ask you something. Just live in the moment. You should do this without trying to change their moods, thoughts, or behavior. You don't need to manage the moment. All you should do is relax and enjoy the time you are spending with your family.

- Cook together

When it comes to hygge, the longer it takes you to make a meal, the better. Foods like soups, stews, comfort foods, and cake are big in hygge. When it comes to hygge time, you can set aside your normal dietary restrictions, within reason, to embrace the foods that you really love. Enjoy the foods that taste good and that you enjoy cooking. The best thing is that this is something you can do with your family as well. Even if you have young children, you can give them something to do to help you fix the meal.

- Enjoy some board games

A great activity for your hygge nights is board games. When you have younger children, this can be a bit harder, but there are board games out there that preschoolers can play. You can even do this as a yearly or monthly game night that you do with friends.

- Take a look through old photos

Hygge is all about creating warm fuzzy feelings. What better way to do that than dragging out some old photo albums and looking through them with your favorite warm beverage? Your kids might even get a kick out of seeing their baby pictures, and even yours. It can even help you remember things that you may not have thought of in a while, and your children will get to see how much they have changed.

- Wear comfortable clothing

When it comes to your hygge night, you're not going to want to wear restrictive clothing. When you're having a hygge night with your family, you can wear your favorite pajamas, yoga pants, sweats, or whatever else you find comfortable so that you are relaxed.

- Enjoy some hot beverages

Hot drinks have an amazing way of creating a cozy environment. For the children, maybe they prefer hot chocolate. You can also enjoy tea, coffee, or cider. Hygge is all about warmth and comfort, so your favorite cold beverage isn't going to cut it. Even the act of making the drink is a great thing to do on a hygge night.

- Get rid of the agenda

Unless your hygge night is on the agenda, forget about everything else you have on the agenda. This night is not when you need to speak with your children about their behavior. This is not the time to bring up things that create anxiety. This is all about spending time with your family. Follow your children. If they want to play another board game, then do it. If they are having a good time being cuddled on the couch and reading a book with you, then continue to do that.

Danish Parenting

Danish parents have six key elements to parenting. Hygge is just something that happens in the process of raising their children. The great thing is, you can easily remember the key elements of Danish parenting by remembering the word PARENT.

P – Play: In Denmark, children get to play independently. This gives them the chance to discover things on their own, work at their own pace, and engage in things that make them happy. While the parent is always there when they need them, they aren't the ones in control of the play.

The act of letting your children play on their own allows them to build up their self-esteem more than doing things that their parents are leading. There is research that has found that play lets children use their creativity while building their imagination. It's also a big part of healthy brain development and leads to more confidence in their capabilities.

A – Authenticity: Danes tend to be more honest with their children about everything. Being authentic and honest with your children helps them build a better internal compass because they learn how to trust their emotions and themselves. While they do praise their children, they avoid empty praise as well as focusing too much on achievements. When you focus a lot on empty praise or achievements, it can cause a child to feel insecure, and they can be afraid of taking risks. Instead, focusing on their effort and accepting all emotions helps them be more secure in their abilities.

R – Reframing: Danish parents will often take some of the more unpleasant moments in life and reframe their perception. This means you shift the focus from the things you can't do to the things you can do. Supporting language teaches you to change the reasons behind actions and emotions, and it will get rid of those tense power struggles. Instead of saying your child is being impossible, try looking at the other side of things. While she may be screaming, crying, and not listening, it is possible she is also bored, tired, hungry, or just needs some love.

Then you can help her get what she wants by using an acceptable behavior. The Danish people do this because they believe that their children are good. Children aren't trying to purposefully make you angry.

E – Empathy: When your child learns how to put themselves into another's shoes, it helps them to be gentler and kinder humans. It is a fundamental value of the Danish people. It is even taught in school there. For an hour every week, students from age six to 16 will be taught empathy. This helps them respect themselves and others and goes a long way to prevent bullying.

N – No Ultimatums: While you may want to physically punish, yell, or threaten your child when they are having a meltdown, the Danish way to do this is taking the diplomatic approach. They avoid ultimatums. Ultimatums are there simply to incite power struggles and form a win-lose relationship between you and your child. They destroy any connection you may have with them, and it does not motivate your child in any way.

For Danish parenting, you want to get rid of threats and replace them with closeness and trust. It leaves your child feeling understood and respected.

T – Togetherness: This is where hygge comes into play. Hygge helps you to build that togetherness with your children, spouse, and friends. This creates a strong sense of community and helps children to feel loved, safe, and happy.

What's Not Hygge Parenting?

While there's not a bunch of hard and fast rules when it comes to hygge parenting, there are some things that hygge parenting isn't. First off, don't bring a bunch of expectations into this hygge time. You can create this vision in your head as to what hygge night will be like, but if you focus on that image, it can cause you to feel dissatisfied with what happens. While your hygge time will need a bit of planning, setting things up, adjusting schedules, and life, it doesn't rely a lot on expectations.

Your main expectation should be the time that you spend with your children.

Avoid letting the outside world into this time. Switch off the TV, phones, and forget about all of the political craziness in the world. Instead, play with your family. Share a meal together. Turn on some music and have a dance party. You could even choose to take a nap together. Whatever you choose to do should give you the chance to focus on the time that you are spending with your family and help those relationships blossom.

Above all, don't cause this to be stressful. That is the exact opposite of what hygge is all about. If hygge is finding that perfect pair of fuzzy slippers, then stressing about it would be like finding a hole in them. Allow this time to simply be family time. It is a great way to take a break from the stress of life and work.

To help you out, here are a few dos and don'ts when it comes to hygge parenting.

1. Don't say, "Now we're really going to hygge" – if you say this, it is going to create too many expectations that can block your hygge night. Hygge isn't something tangible that you can grab hold of. It is something that simply occurs at the moment, so you can't stage it.
2. Do leave all of your drama at the door. There is going to be plenty of time to focus on any issues that you could be having. Hygge is more concerned with creating a safe space for your family to relax.
3. Don't use your tablets or your phones. Switch them

off and place them in a different room. When you provide your children with your full attention, you make the time you have with them a lot easier.
4. Do fit hygge night into your daily or weekly routine. This will help to make your children feel safe, and they will associate it with something comfortable and nice.
5. Do work to create a cozy atmosphere for your hygge night. Having some candles, baking a cake, and playing some games are great ways to do this. A big part of hygge begins with preparing for your night with the family.

The Benefits

As you begin practicing hygge with your family, one of the biggest benefits of this is the serenity and calmness that it brings to your family. Besides that, you'll notice that everybody is a lot happier and optimistic. Who wouldn't want to have happier children?

With these hygge sessions, the overall wellbeing of children can be improved. Mental health has a huge role in a person's wellbeing. There is a lot of research that has found that spending quality time with people we care about brings us more happiness, more so than anything else in life. It also gives you a chance to practice mindfulness as you work on living in the moment as you spend time with your family.

One of the best things about bringing hygge into parenting is the bond that you build with your kids. All of you will be more connected, more aware of one another, even outside of them. It will create a more secure feeling in the home, creating a safe place from the world. There is a lot of negativity that children can be faced with on a daily basis, and this can help give them a safe place to go where they know the negativity won't follow.

When you take the time to incorporate hygge into your family life, you provide your children with the home base that they need to deal with the harder things in life. As your relationship and bond with them grows, you'll create a foundation that will bring you a lifelong closeness that will be more satisfying and valuable than anything else.

six
hygge throughout the year

HYGGE ISN'T something that can only be practiced during the winter. It is something that you can bring into your life all year round. You can bring hygge into all of your holidays and celebrations you have throughout the year.

Hygge Birthdays

So your birthday may be in the middle of summer, or it could be in the dead of winter, but you could still throw a hygge inspired birthday party. All you have to do is bring the coziness and togetherness that hygge is all about into your party. Let's go over some ways to throw a hygge birthday party.

First, figure out what kind of foods you want. Remember, hygge is big on comfort foods. Think pies, cakes, casseroles, chili, soup, mac N cheese, popcorn, anything that you like and find comforting. You can also make it buffet style so that people can dress up their food however they want. A taco bar could be a good choice.

. . .

Then you have the beverages. While hygge is big into warm beverages, if your birthday does fall in the middle of summer, that might not be the best option. In that case, you could choose to go with some cold. You can also go with your favorite adult beverages if you are inviting only adults.

With that in mind, let's go over nine more tips to make your birthday perfectly hygge.

- Set the mood with the right lighting

It has been said before, but hygge is all about lighting. Make use of natural lighting if you have any at the time of your party. You can also use candles, twinkly lights, or anything that gives you just enough light to see what's going on. You don't want it too bright.

- Keep the party casual

While most of us enjoy getting fancied up from time to time, your hygge birthday is not the time for that. Ensure your party guests know that the dress code is super casual. Whatever the season-appropriate casual attire is, dress in that. If it's cold, wear cozy boots, a large sweater, and some leggings, gentleman can swap the leggings for a comfy pair of sweatpants. If it's the summer, maybe you choose a floppy tank top and some shorts and flip-flops.

- Pick the right guests

When it comes to your hygge birthday party, it's not about inviting everybody you know and having your party be the talk of the town. Instead, you want to focus on inviting the people that you care about the most. Invite your closest family and friends for your relaxed party. Think about how each person's personality will work with everybody else's. Hygge is also a great thing for introverts, so you may just be able to invite that friend that's not big on parties with a promise of a relaxed evening in.

- Comforting sounds

Hygge parties are all about conversation and togetherness, so you don't need the latest hits drowning out everybody. However, a little background noise is a great thing to have to smooth over any lulls that the conversation may have. Some jazz music or Nordic sounds are great. Spotify has a lot of pre-made playlists that would work well.

- Enjoy some light conversations

It can sometimes seem impossible to have a conversation with people without the topics of politics coming up. However, your hygge party is not the time for that kind of conversation. If the conversation starts to take a controversial turn, bring it back to something light-hearted and fun. You could even bring out party games. This will help to keep the feel of the party light and comfortable and avoid those awkward moments.

- Bring the outside in

Bring some pretty floral bouquets to your home to help decorate for the party. That's really all of the decoration you will need for your party. Pick out your favorite flowers, and place a couple of arrangements in your home.

- It's all about moderation

Sometimes hearing that hygge is about comfort food, people think that means you have to overindulge as well, but that's not true. There is a Swedish term, "lagom," which roughly translates to "just the right amount." That's what you should always be aiming for when it comes to hygge. Don't get the third serving just because the party is a hygge party. You want the food to satisfy everybody, not leave everybody feeling bloated and uncomfortable. Foods that people can graze on are a good idea.

- Find a relaxing spot

It's all about cozy and comfy, right? You're going to need a place where everybody can come together and relax. Have a bunch of cushions, blankets, pillows, and more in your living room so everybody can fix themselves a comfy little nest chill in. Having the drinks and food in that same area will make the evening go more smoothly.

- Don't panic

If something were to go wrong, a person spills their drink, or the bread burns, try not to panic. People like to describe hygge as "the absence of all things irritating, annoying, or stressful," so don't let the little things throw you into a tizzy. It's not the end of the world. Clean up the mess and turn your focus back to your guests, and bring you all together to celebrate your day of birth.

Hygge and the Holidays

The holidays are right around the corner, and most people are looking for more comfort this year. Many people have found that you can find joy and coziness that comes with the holidays in their home.

The holidays for me have been about bringing warmth and coziness into my home. So bringing hygge into the holidays won't be too hard for me, but if you aren't used to this, you will find some tips below. Hygge is all about bringing comfort, coziness, and friendliness into the home to make everyone feel well and content. If you are ready, let's get started.

- Be Mindful

Hygge has one important element, and that is mindfulness. You aren't going to be able to enjoy the contentment and coziness while you are mindlessly scrolling through your social media pages. You have to be aware and present while disconnecting from the things happening around you. You need to encourage the entire family to do this too.

- Blankets

You can't have hygge if you don't have blankets to curl up under on cold days. You are going to have lots of opportunities to do this if you can add more blankets throughout your house. Children are going to love all the chances to build a fort out of all the blankets lying around. They also love cuddling with you under a blanket while you read them a book or watch a movie.

- Quality Time

Most of the old family traditions around the holidays have been pushed aside by all the commercialism. You can change this. Find more quality time rather than buying gifts. Just notice the way your family's attitude will change during the holidays. They will soon be looking forward to all the magic this season brings.

- Go Outside

Having a hygge holiday can't exist if you remain inside. You have to go outside and enjoy all the magic that the holidays bring. Once you come back inside, you can make some hot cocoa and enjoy it while thawing out in front of the fire. Having fun outside and loving nature is the fun you need before you enjoy the cozy.

- Light A Fire

Many people are lucky and have fireplaces. But they might not know how to use it. It is extremely important that you know what you are doing before you light a fire in your house. Go over all the safety rules with your children and significant others and use the fireplace every chance you get. It will add an extremely cozy element to any house.

- Candles

It doesn't matter if you have a fireplace or not; candles are essential. Candles can add ambiance, warmth, and another element to the festivities. With all the warm blankets and some candles, you will have a hygge home in no time.

- Get Creative with Drinks and Meals

You have to go above and beyond your normal meals during the holiday season. Warm, delicious drinks and large meals are the way to have a hygge and happy belly. Get out the cookbooks or do an online search for dishes you've never made before. You just don't know when you will discover your newest tradition.

- Read Your Favorite Book

Swap your tablet, phone, and television for a good book to help you find your inner peace. You might have several new titles on your reading list that you haven't found the time to read just yet. This hygge holiday is the perfect time to begin that list.

Christmas

Just getting into the spirits of the holidays is a good way to feel positive in this crazy world that has been turned upside down for the past years. With all the social distancing and shutdowns, we have been forced to slow down a lot. We need to return to a simpler holiday.

This year, for the holidays, you have to release all your expectations. Release all those expectations from all the ghosts of Christmases past. Once you can let go of all your expectations, you can focus on all the good. This needs to come from inside you as nobody can make a mindset change but you.

You need to be ready to embrace these changes and make the most of every situation. If you are ready, bringing hygge into your home for the holidays is a lot easier than you might think. Here are a few ideas that can help you make it happen.

- Save Money

Don't have any parties and don't go to the movies. This one might be hard, but if your office participates in a "Secret Santa" gift exchange, bow out of it this year. You are going to save some money which might help with the way the world is right now.

- Calmness and Peace

Everyone loves having a good party with many people around us. Calmness and peace is a wonderful time to reenergize and recharge yourself.

- Time

Who in this world doesn't need a few more hours in our day? This isn't the time I'm talking about. Stop rushing around and take some time to look in local shops for gifts rather than just ordering them from Amazon. Take some time to have a family movie night and watch the old Christmas movies. Take some time and do some baking. Homemade gifts are sometimes the best gifts you can give.

In this section, I will share some great Hygge traditions to help you slow down and enjoy all the simple things in life.

Just like having a gratitude attitude and mindfulness, hygge is how you look at life that only focuses on the simple pleasures while taking time to make more of them in your life. It is the time to give your spirit, mind, and body some time to rest while you enjoy all the good things in life like watching the sunset or sunrise, reading your favorite book, drinking a mug of your favorite tea or coffee, and spending as much time with the people you love in a comfy environment.

Rather than living your life on autopilot, incorporating hygge into your life can help you make sure you are living your life in ways that will bring you contentment deep in your soul.

. . .

There are times when things in your life like achievements, power, and money aren't all the things that are going to make you happy. Having a hygge life will help you look at what will really bring you joy, so you have to make sure you add these things into your days.

- Natural Decorations

Incorporating natural elements when creating your cozy space during the Christmas season is essential. Natural colors and vibrant greens bring the outside indoors. Using old craftsmanship is getting a revival. Use grasses, bark, seed bulbs, and dried flowers and combine these with metals. This is a good way to remain on budget while decorating. If you love getting crafty, this is a great way to bring hygge into your Christmas.

- Never Forget

Put pictures of your loved ones who have passed in small frames and put them on your mantle. Add some evergreen around them. This symbolizes eternal life. You could put the pictures in ornament frames and put them on your tree. Remember to tell your children stories about these passed loved ones, so their memories live through the generations.

- Movie Night

Put aside one day to be a movie marathon. Get everything ready and get comfortable to watch all the classic Christmas movies that we all know and love. Create a hot chocolate bar, put piles of blankets and pillows on the floor, and have the pizza in the oven.

- Secret Santa

Yes, I know I told you to forget the "Secret Santa" at work, but this is using "Secret Santa" with family. Put everybody's name in a bowl and have everyone draw a name, and this is their "Secret Santa." This idea is doing nice things for whoever's name you drew without getting caught. You aren't going to buy them a present; you are only going to do nice things for them. When you have your Christmas Eve dinner, everybody has to guess who their "Secret Santa" was. If someone guesses correctly, have a small gift for them. Once everyone has had a guess, you can let them reveal who they were "Secret Santa" for.

- Holiday Windows

Put every family member in charge of decorating one window. Have a contest and give prizes to the person who was most creative. They can choose to decorate the window, or if there is a ledge that they can reach, they could choose to decorate that too.

- Ornaments That Have A History

I love Christmas ornaments and try to buy a new one each year to add to the tree. Each year we have a lot of fun unpacking them and then remembering where we got them. Every ornament will tell a different story and has a life all of its own. If you want to add more depth to your tree, add ornaments that represent an interest or passion, world events that meant something to the family, professional or personal milestones. The year my daughter graduated from college, I bought her one that represented the theatre and had it personalized with her name. I bought my husband one that said "Mr. Fix It" since he is the "Mr. Fix It" in our house. Get creative and have some fun.

- Matching PJs

You can celebrate being a family by buying the entire family matching pajamas to wear on Christmas Eve. You can find these in most stores these days. Buy them early because if you wait until they go on sale, you might be too late.

- Christmas Dishes

I'm not talking food here, but the food is a big part of the hygge Christmas. Have a set of Christmas dishes that have Christmas scenes on them and begin using them on December 1st and continue using them until Christmas Day. You can buy a whole set of the same design or get creative and buy a piece at a time at thrift stores until you have enough for your table setting.

- Christmas Camping

Allow your children to sleep under the tree in sleeping bags. Turn off the lights except for the tree and read your child's favorite Christmas story.

I absolutely love the idea of adding hygge traditions to my Christmas season. This is the perfect year to start this process. I want everyone reading this book to have safety, love, and peace during their holiday season.

seven
clothing

FASHION POLICE, I'd like to introduce you to hygge. This is how the Danes look at being extremely comfortable and cozy. This new fashion trend has taken the world by storm. Interior design isn't safe from this ancient concept. Fluffy pillows and blankets sell out in a matter of minutes when they hit the salesroom floor. Mugs the size of cantaloupes are filled with ginger tea, and conversations are endless. If your friends are anything like mine, they can't quit talking about hygge and making their homes into a hygge paradise. In this world of chaos, everybody wants to walk into their house that has been transformed into a fluffy paradise.

But hygge doesn't have to just apply to the inside of your house. You can actually bring hygge into anything you want. You can hygge your tea. You can hygge your cocktails. You can even hygge your activities in any season. But for those fashion police, you can even hygge your wardrobe.

The biggest concepts at the heart of hygge fashion will include something called "top bulky" (we'll get into that more in a minute), lots of black, woolen socks, and scarves. These sound easy, right, but try to layer all your black clothes "top bulky" and just watch what happens. Instead of trying to do that, here are some suggestions to get your personal style "hyggeified" while remaining true to each season.

- Knits From Top to Bottom

The most crucial concept for hygge is being comfortable. What could be more comfortable than wearing knit clothing from your head to your toes? Stella McCartney and Victoria Beckham modeled knitwear during the fall fashion show back in 2017.

- Fluffy Socks

If you want to be in true hygge fashion, you have to purchase some wooly socks. You can pair them with cropped pants, loafers, and a big furry jacket. You might even find a pair of slippers that are lined with fur. Even though there hasn't been anything said about slide sandals, I'm sure hygge would still approve.

- Scarves and More Scarves

To the more fashionable people out there, you might be thinking that the skinny scarves went out with Heidi Slimane's Saint Laurent and the larger bulkier scarves are too passé, but you can shake it up with some knitted ones that match your clothes or just knot one around your neck.

- Layers and Lots of Them

The more layers you have on, the better. If you are staying home, you can try layering with a pair of woolen socks, a pair of leggings, a pair of cropped pants, a sweatshirt, and top it off with a bomber jacket. If you are going out, you can add layers under a dress with some tights and leggings. Don't forget to add your jacket and a scarf before you head out the door.

- Black is Well Everything

Hygge can be about wearing all black. Just don't forget to layer and remember that "top bulky." This basically means putting an oversized coat on top of everything else. You will have to buy this about two sizes larger than you normally wear since you are putting other clothing under it.

- Buy a Sweater Sarah Lund Would Wear

If you don't know who Sarah Lund is, she is a character in a television drama called The Killing. This sweater is so popular in Denmark that factories can't produce enough of them. As soon as they get into stores, they are sold out in seconds. Joseph and Victoria Beckham have created some sweaters that resemble Lund's look if you can find them.

- If You Have To Leave Your House, Stay Warm

Hygge loves dressing casually. If you have to get all gussied up, try to figure out how you can stay warm while toning down the glitz factor. Topping off your look with a fluffy sweater or jacket is an absolute must.

- Coordinating Your Fashion with Your House's Interior

The heart of hygge is trying to remain inside and getting through those cold winter months the best you can. When you are in, you could find a way to make your looks match those of your interior. Try matching your clothing with some of your artwork on your walls, or match your dress with your couch.

Picking the Best Clothes for a Hygge Winter

If you grew up in Denmark, you would have been told, "there's isn't a thing as bad weather, only the clothing that isn't suitable." This basically means you need to put on "your rain gear, and go outside" or "to bundle in layers and go outside?"

I recently moved from "the land of eternal summer," which is Florida, to Washington, which is the "land of eternal rain." In Washington, winter is just around the corner, and it is already getting darker faster. Going barefoot to get the mail can't be done until late spring now.

I decided to use my Danish ancestry and embrace hygge in my house since it is getting cold outside. Even though I am trying my best to live my life in rainy, cold Washington states, I have been able to find some very stylish and comfortable clothing. I can wear these while sitting by the fire, on a coffee date with friends, taking a walk out in nature (if you're brave enough), or spending the evening playing games with the family.

Whatever you can think of doing, you can do it in any of these clothes I have listed below to embrace hygge with your family and friends.

As you have figured out by now, hygge is a lifestyle if you live in Denmark. Danes have constantly ranked as "the happiest people in the whole world," and this is all because of how they live. If you think about hygge, just think about being happy in fluffy, comfortable clothes.

I love pairing a comfy pair of leggings or yoga pants with a half zip hoodie because nothing is better than comfortable yoga pants and a warm hoodie. I have been known to wear leggings or yoga pants all over town doing anything. They hug you in all the right places without getting constricting or too tight.

Hoodies are great, too. You can layer them under a bigger coat to watch outdoor ball games without going into hypothermic shock. Okay, so it might not be that cold out just yet, but it is fairly chilly. Hoodies look great alone, too.

While you are looking for your hygge clothes to get you through winter, try to find these features:

- Comfort

Hygge is all about being cozy, comfortable, and effortless. There shouldn't be any worrying or stressing when you are in hygge. When you are in your hygge pants, you should never have to worry when you bend over that you are going to show your "plumbers' crack" or you have to constantly suck in your stomach. Your shirts shouldn't be tight or flash everything you have. Hygge clothes should be comfortable and stylish, and this is whatever stylish means to you.

- Tiny Patterns

No huge tropical flowers or bright colors; you can wear small, delicate flowers but no bold patterns or prints.

- Soft Fabrics and Natural Materials

Most hygge clothes are usually made from linen, cotton, and wool. They need to be soft without worrying about creases or wrinkles.

- Layers

When you embrace hygge, you will be embracing coziness and comfort. Warm socks, oversized shawls or scarves, layers of clothing that just scream hygge.

- Neutral, Muted Colors

Hygge is all about being mild, soft, nothing crass or bright, and this carries over to your colors selection, too.

How to Dress Like a Dane

As the year moves forward to the approaching winter season, now is the time to embrace hygge. You can do this in how you dress and how you live. Let's see how to dress like a Dane.

- More Quality Less Quantity

Danes are known for the "capsule wardrobe." This basically means you have just a few quality pieces of clothing to work well together, as opposed to having a closet full of mismatched clothes that you never wear. Try to find pieces that are made from all-natural materials.

- Earthy, Monochromatic Tones

We've already covered this one a bit, but Danes wear colors that are inspired by nature. Their wardrobe will have many earthy tones and lots of blacks. This can help you create a well-coordinated, functional wardrobe that you can easily work with. You can use black as your base to make a minimalistic, sleek style that they are known for.

- Cozy Textures and Relaxed Silhouettes

Hygge living is about making a peaceful, cozy environment. Any type of clothing that isn't practical or is uncomfortable isn't welcome. Danes love beautiful textures and relaxed silhouettes to make a comfortable but minimalistic vibe. Try to envision oversized knits, relaxed dresses, and wide-legged pants.

- Quality but Practical Footwear

Most people in Denmark ride their bicycles everywhere they go, so they need very practical shoes. During winter, this means they need some waterproof shoes that keep their feet warm and toasty.

During summer, you can change into a white sneaker or sandals without heels. These would be great for an afternoon at the park with friends.

- White, Crisp Shirts

This might be the most fundamental item in Dane's wardrobe; a classic, white shirt that is comfortable. It is minimalist and can be paired with anything. You can dress it down or up.

- Hats

You absolutely have to have a warm hat. Most people don't realize that they lose most of their body temperature through their heads. No, wearing a hat doesn't do anything for your hairstyle, but it is going to keep you warm. So if you live where it is bitter cold, a hat is a must. Make sure to stay with the muted, earthy tones. If you can find a wool hat with a fleece lining, you are in business.

- Mittens

Gloves are fine if you are going to be using a camera and taking pictures, but if you are just out and about, mittens will keep your hands warmer. If you can find some that are lined with fleece and fit well around your wrist, they will keep the water, snow, and wind out so nothing can get in and make your fingers cold.

If you can't find waterproof mittens, you can do it yourself with a can of "Scotch Guard." All you have to do is follow the directions on the can.

- Scarf

Yes, this has been covered, but I love scarves. I have tons in various colors, and the wider and longer, the better so you can wrap them around your neck many times. Try to find some that are made from wool or a natural fiber that will keep you toasty and warm. If you can wrap it so that it is inside your jacket, the better to keep your neck and chest warm.

- Cozy Socks

If you aren't allergic to wool, it is a must to keep your feet warm. Never put on cotton socks if your feet are going to get wet. Having a pair of wool socks that can be pulled up to your knees is ideal. They can keep your feet and legs warm, and you can let them peek above your boots for another stylish look. Just a quick note, men's wool socks are priced lower and are of better quality than women's.

- Warm Coat

This might sound too obvious to you, but your average coat just isn't going to cut it when you are trying to hygge. If where you live gets windy or extremely cold, you probably need to find something extremely warm and thick.

A good, warm winter coat is worth the money you will spend on it as it will get you through several winters without having to buy another one. You could opt for a down-filled jacket that is stylish and cute.

If you don't want to have to sell an important organ, or you want something for hiking during the winter, you can find a waterproof jacket, a parka, or a coat from North Face. Most of these jackets stay in style, and they last you a very long time.

If you aren't going to be spending a lot of time in extreme temperatures, these might be a bit too expensive. Try to find a good, warm coat that you know will keep you warm, and then layer it if you have to.

- Boots

If you live where it is rainy or snowy, you absolutely need a pair of waterproof boots. Your mornings might consist of rain, mist, or frost that will melt into slush. You might encounter puddles or ice, and if it snows, your main priority is to have a pair of waterproof boots.

You might want to go one more step and make sure they have been lined with something warm, like fleece or fur.

- Long Underwear

If you are going to be out in the weather a lot, these are a must-have. These could literally save your life. Invest in a good pair of long johns, and you won't ever feel cold while out in the weather. You can find great ones on Amazon that are good quality and won't cost you an arm and a leg.

I'm talking both top and bottom pieces here. Most people don't think about the top part since they will be wearing a jacket, but if you are going to be in the wind, they are a must.

- Sweaters

Yes, talked about these already, too, but they are essential. This goes over the long underwear but under the coat. Having lots of sweaters is essential. Just remember to keep them in the earthy tones.

Cashmere sweaters are a bit more expensive, but they are well worth the investment.

- Pants But Not Jeans

The main thing that most people do wrong is wearing denim. Jeans actually hold the cold in and even if you have long underwear under them. Your legs are going to get extremely cold.

Rather than wearing jeans, think about getting some wool pants or knit pants that you can layer. Flannel knit pants would be great too. They are warm without being constricting, and you can layer tights, long underwear, or other leggings underneath.

afterword

Thank you for making it through to the end of *The Hygge Book*; let's hope it was informative and able to provide you with all of the tools you need to achieve your goals, whatever they may be.

The next step is to start implanting some of your favorite hygge practices into your life. There really isn't a right or wrong way to do that. Find what you feel is comfortable and what you enjoy. That's what hygge is all about. Bringing hygge into every aspect of your life is fairly simple to do. It can even improve your relationships and how you parent. The possibilities are endless for your hygge life.

Finally, if you found this book useful in any way, a review is always appreciated!

Further Reading
    Go check out my other books where I'm exploring life happiness and purpose in other countries:

The Ikigai Book: Finding Happiness and Purpose the Japanese way.

The Lagom Book: A Balanced and Happy Life from Sweden.